AF439581

stled within the pages lies a profound journey unlike any other. Vincent, a soulful writer who sitates to don the title of poet, possesses an otherworldly gift for words that transcends mere ose. From the depths of his being, his writing emerges, wielding a power that resonates with ound emotional intensity. Each carefully crafted word bears a weighty significance, reflecting his unique perspective and lived experiences.

cent's path has been intertwined with the haunting shadow of post-traumatic stress disorder (PTSD), an indelible mark etched onto the fabric of his existence. Yet, he navigates this reacherous terrain, stripped of a reliable support system. The dearth of confidants and the sence of a consistent therapist thrust him into a battle against his inner demons alone. The sient nature of fleeting connections in his past, individuals who departed after a mere week or two, only served to intensify his isolation and deepen the wounds he carries.

Childhood for Vincent was a tempestuous and agonizing era, marred by both physical and ental abuse. His room, once a sanctuary for many, offered him little solace. There, his father l stepmother callously subjected him to frequent "sweeps," stripping away his possessions and aving behind an overwhelming sense of emptiness and vulnerability. Amidst the chaos, they riously spared a single item—the red dictionary. This seemingly mundane object became a bol of the fragments of his identity that remained intact, a lifeline that connected him to self-expression and testified to his unwavering resilience.

It is in the depths of his triggered emotions that Vincent's writing truly awakens. When the painful memories of his past resurface, his words take flight, soaring beyond the confines of rdinary language. Each sentence becomes a masterful brushstroke on the canvas of his pain, aving a poignant tapestry of his experiences. Through his writing, he peels back the layers of trauma, embracing vulnerability and transforming his suffering into a profound work of art.

ess than ten minutes, Vincent's words spin a spellbinding tapestry that surprises and captivates eaders. With profound depth and eloquence, he beckons others into his world—a world of guish, survival, and an unwavering quest for inner peace. Through his writing, he seeks solace himself and connection with those who resonate with his journey, offering a beacon of hope to ow travelers who have faced their own trials and tribulations. And all of this unfolds within the ges, a vessel that holds the power to transport readers to the realms of Vincent's extraordinary narrative.

The echoes of the story, forever changed its wisdom,
The profound truths unveiled.
Hearts brimming with gratitude,
They stepped into their own narratives, inspired to embrace their own
adventures,
Armed with the knowledge that
The realms of fiction lie in the power.
The power that shapes our reality.
Yet, to ignite the courage
Is to live your own extraordinary stories.

Introduction

The world he once lived in had sad moments, people who would come and leave, places and things that evoker painful memories, and flashes of tragedy from his childhood, love stories, and friendships. Eventually, he collapsed.

Later, he woke up and said, "It's time for this heavy storm to finally pass. But how?" It starts with the exploration of the past. Then remembrance. And lastly the choice between fight or flight. Follow the journey of a once-troubled questioning soul that wandered through hurricanes, tornadoes, and floods. That left behind nothing but damaged homes, damaged buildings, and damaged mindsets.

Reading starts...

Reflect and Chill.

Who you are today is a reflection of some kind of memory.

~~Love~~

~~Lust~~

~~Trust~~

~~Confidence~~

His next step involves a conflict.
The written work on himself.
Should I stay or should I go?

Travel through your past. Think of the People, Places, and Things that
have
Left scars. Now think about
How and why a scar will not disappear.

TRIGGERS

Loud noise

Yelling

Crowds

People behind

Fighting (being involved in or seeing)

Scenic views

Post office

It began with becoming an analyst and drowning in every type of data that comes to mind.
He realized he was not accurate at all.
No matter how much he tried. A permanent defect had been discovered.

"A subtle way of looking at the future
With hope"

"Eye roll" Finger tapping

The storms are brewing. A catastrophic disaster will take place...ride it out.

in distress

Drugged

High on life? Chill.

Overwhelming offers and overwhelming joys?

It's to trick you into thinking you're an impulsive idiot.

Director wanted

The scene:
'When good things happen'

His part: a narcissist

The ending:
Lost connections
New scars
Timeline maker
Repeated patterns
Encountering enemies, situations, and things.
You took an emotional ride back to the past, to the scars on the brain.

You asked why your fears of everyday living became the norm.
It lasted for so long.
Then time expired. The people, places,
And things all left.

Someone took away my self-worth.

Intimacy was not consensual.

You just became the victim of an already

Hard journey. Damaged setting.

Fuck man

Turn away from him. His voice, face, and eyes bear weakness.

He hasn't seen himself.

He avoids the mirrors he comes across.

Fuck man feeling worthless

After an intimacy without consent. Definitely a...

Froze.

Arrive stronger than yesterday, learn how to leave gracefully

---

Unfortunately, he wished for the past to go away.

A smell a touch a look

Formed a destructive path while moving forward.

Pay attention to the scar. Figure out a coping mechanism.

Key points

Environment

Company

You

12
A
Personal Defect

A big sigh

...every time.

Ok grandma

"Is it hard to not be emotional? Maybe challenge yourself? Don't be
senseless, be sensitive. It'll only hurt you."

Sponge

Take the time to read the inside to understand that you'll always be
wrong.

Company that he once kept
"A never-ending cycle of battles
A never-ending emotional roller coaster
Ride
Drama filled scenes turning into present day confusions, déjà vus, and
puzzling nights."

Daily routine: wrongful company, still continues...

Hope: is change a possibility?

The People?
The Places?
The Things?
Storyline: Your past leaves scars, dents, scraps, laughter, and subtle cries.
The present gives lessons, guides, and teaches patience and practice.

The future your present day past errors revisited into a teaching lesson. Of some kind of new emotional or physical scenario. Created by you, or by others.

The end.
Prepared, scared, and ready?

Note to self:
Trauma is a permanent, yet painful and draining internal process for others around you.

Company

Inhaling every word spoken, turning it into the language of strength, wisdom, and glory.

Crayons

Pursue a gifted talent, be the mind, be the vision, be the stigma, and the rave. Trust the first thought, and always stop at five rewrites.

How to balance: him
~~Restraint~~
~~Love~~
~~Lust~~
~~Leader~~
~~Respect~~

The glass is filled. What's next?

He dozes off to a deep sleep, but is woken up by a loud unfamiliar noise. He creeps past the curtain and sees a spaceship, waiting for him outside. Confused, he grabs his coat and rushes out the door. When he arrives at the spacecraft, he hears in the background. "Come my dear son, let's review your timeline." Frozen, scared, his heart sinking, he murmurs, "Who said that?" Waiting for a reply…He is awakened by the morning rays of the sun. Puzzled and confused, he keeps on repeating, "I swear I was there. But whose was that voice?" His morning continues: routines, familiar faces, repeated moments, and tragic flashbacks. With a cup of coffee, he settles into his living-room couch. Turns on the daily news. His mind begins to wander back to the morning's confusion. "Who said that?" The process of wondering creates billions

Of scenes, characters, and themes that have zero relevance at all. He shrugs his shoulders, gets up, and
Continues with his day. "Hopefully, a repeat won't crop up. That was tiring..." his mind turns down the volume.

The mirror you are avoiding just became your first smile of the day.

Steps of a PTSD attack: Patient: HIM

Your personal preference is interfering with someone's life—overthink

Flap those wings, as if you're the greatest of them all—the ego reminder

The silent storm—the brain begins to overthink

Breaks down—freezes, shakes, and walks away

In emotional distress—the "fight or flight"

Reminder to self—you are the greatest of them all

Reminder to self—you are the strongest of them—chooses to fight

Gains control—back in order

26

Taylor Swift's love story
Emo key hummingbird heart
Emotionless euphoric lust

"My forgotten king I beg to be your queen, I beg to rule your kingdom
beside you night and day
My forgotten king?
Your gifts and wisdom that turned into euphoric lust, what happened?
My forgotten king
Why can't you see my love no more?"

Forgotten king (nonu)—the first lover.
The rain will begin to come down a river melody is heard in the
background
A sentimental feeling has occurred

The mood filled with joy, happiness, and love.

A desire. A goal.

The law of attraction.

To settle on a treaty a war needs to start

A mental breakdown

A tag along emotional journey is becoming your traumatized experience

To be continued...

The rocky paths are clearing. The clouds are scattering away.

The sun is beginning to rise over the horizon to create the clearing for something new

Admit

You are the ticking time bomb in everyone's eyes. You create your own misery.

Lol.

Rain on my parade

The day of the parade was dark, cloudy, and dreary. As if you had control the whole time? They just assumed you did. To assume is to think one is powerless,
And to assume is to be an automatic liar.
):

Mentally drained

He fought the feeling of ending his life. He was confused as to why and how others would just give up on their memories. He questioned why others were swarming in and out of his life?

:/

Photographs
He reflects on a time that changed his soul
The band-aid can be lifted now
Let's see if he's strong enough.

Second part

The coursework
He's coming back.
The old entrepreneur will be open soon.
He's just closed now.

Not a favorable view

He glides into the future with stop and yield signs. He slows down with caution Then proceeds with anger and rage. The memories start to form, it's not easy to let go.

One.

A success story will hurt a lot of people a goal for yourself will become a
guilty habit that will underestimate your ability
You then become a product of a producer.
When do you ever learn?

Learning to be confident in a situation without having a mental
breakdown is the next step of self-growth
A mind-shocker moment. The last part reads...

Confused over scenarios

He is in an emotional state; his body is numb to its surroundings, and clueless to his actions. Repairing an old wound opened up the possibility of finding a cure to his overthinking.

You're going to belittle my abilities. The storm will start to form.
I'll make it rain, first as a warning. The voice will get higher as the clouds become darker, and thunder and lightning will start to strike to complete the course of action.
If you cut deep enough into a conversation, medical attention will be needed. Your mindset need not be portrayed. The problem is you. You are hard-headed and not self-aware.
If you cut deep enough into a conversation, medical attention is needed.

The days you waste are considered pointless

Reread your day over and over again.
A pointless day is a forgotten course.

Rich man's drug

He almost won this night, the phantom taste of perception, the smoke

that brought him out in the first place

Soon arose to my soul

Tricking me into thinking it's okay, just this one time,

I wanted to get aroused

With some stranger I didn't know, with the act of wanting to taste the

smoke

He almost won this night

A test from the higher power, seeing the abilities I have to offer during

their visit

In this chapter, I call my given chance

He almost won this night

Shook Weary

Even worse, considering the worst for the future
Realizing I have to admit to someone, guiding me through the journey of
this course,
I caught within myself
A test from my higher power during their visit
In this chapter, I call my given chance
He didn't win today
Let's hope tomorrow he does with the same mentality
Oui

Sometimes he lets his weak mind take over his conversations.
He fucked up with a lot, which he can't seem to accept
While exploding with the emotions of unfortunate events he's created
The wars of the past bloody days will

Forever be a scar, a permanent memory, and a heartache burden.

A different kind of soul that walks with, a dweller

A rusher a runaway

Not allowing any type of advice, yet relying on the only thought from

oneself. His ego is taking charge

Impulsive desires are showing

He was trying hard to forget about the bloody war

He took the steps to try to clean up

All this only put him in emotional distress.

You only got you

The restless nights are creeping in. The restless night clouds are starting to
cover a once star-lit sky.
Covering a full moon that once shined so bright, unafraid of the storms
that might be coming
The restless nights are creeping in. Once a star-lit sky,
Now a prediction of catastrophic events
As he waits for the threat of danger Do I have to run?
Do I have to hide? Do I ride it out?
A once starlit sky
Now he faces the fears of danger

47

Going for the next goal is a hard moment

The drive

The ambition

The changes

The loss of others

Even the negative reviews

Can be a war before reaching that goal

Today has already happened

That doesn't mean

Tomorrow hasn't already begun to brew

Yesterday you didn't reach for that goal Tomorrow will be the same

Remember the last night you were restless

Remember the negative reviews

It'll only drive your ambition further

Just for today

Follow the yellow brick road

It'll lead into something more

Than it did yesterday

49

"When the timeless efforts of trying to win the hearts of others fail, it is
A forever mental note for the books. As the course begins, the learning of
Yourself will be profound in the eyes of others.
Learn the self-care ritual
Of loving yourself, building yourself,
And creating your ways of saying of no."

Written in three parts, with the same key

I am the power of my universe I am the mogul of my name
I am the past of my future abilities
While making a name for changes I am the mogul of my name
I am the hero too of my story
Feeling mentally unstable after leaving the bloody trails of the broken wars
i've had within myself
Daily doses of reminders of owning my past
My intentions are pure
Are you ready for this mogul to become the next success story?
A mind once dictated by the company he kept, the eyes of the devil was
seen at a quick glance

His higher power found him first. Guided him toward finding unspoken
details
I am the power of my universe I am the mogul of my name
I am the past of my future abilities While surpassing the worst mindset
gliding over time, he once said, "I am the best of them all."
Getting closer to the truth,
Become willing to process. I am the joke of the group.
Your mindset is so easily persuaded, you burst into complete anger
Completely lost while trying to find the right shelter
Losing friends
Losing people that are actually trying to be in your future
A traumatized mind

The unwillingness, the feeling of emptiness, the feeling of never being able

to trust.

This traumatized mindset should rest now; today isn't the day he dies, this

so- called life change

Of happy highs and low endings

Destroying your mind for a day's worth of living

Facing the mirrors where you once saw a complete success story, now a

destroyed soul

That wants to refuse the opportunity of becoming a new person

Holding on to the thoughts of relapsing

Why?

Ego. It has got to him.

The person he once created,

Is trying to overpower his past by turning it into present day trauma,

Reliving past scars

Completely swamped in a puddle of tears, this feeling of a destroyed past

Changes you.

Begging for some kind of happiness, while he loses his "a man's best

friend" Lonely

Terrified

Completely forgot what it's like to trust a person that follows him into a

room.

They're seeking the same kind of treatment he is.

Little does he know the type of people he once called his friends.

A plot twist all too normal.

The devil is trying to make his way back. He is allowing it.

Help his soul.

He can't even face mirrors anymore without wanting to create endless

waterfalls,

As if they exist in his universe.

Happy moments joyful moments humbling moments
A bittersweet statement that'll bring a lot more than just happiness
It's a kind of plot twist. Sick, right?
Remember the phenomenon you once were,
Remember the burden you brought upon yourself
After hearing that
If tomorrow doesn't happen, you must change it.
You must make tomorrow happen. Remember you're more worthy than
that

Piece of what the devil wants you to put into the body.

If tomorrow doesn't happen, you'll know why.

Here

If you're going to doubt him with an ignorant remark,
Why continue with this manner of respecting him?
Your energy is not a plot twist to him, it's more of a feast for him.
He can be as evil as you. Don't swarm him with a sorry,
He will end up laughing with the higher power watching over him
Definitely knows his self-worth.
Don't underestimate his recovery process by saying, "You'll end up with
the devil again"
Because a relapse won't be on his agenda anytime soon.
Your energy is not a plot twist to him, it's more of a feast for him
So watch what you serve.

He will end up eating it up with a proud smile.

Read the signs that'll bring grace and harmony back into your universe.

Read the signs that'll help you become prouder during your review of the next chapter.

Read the signs that'll help you work on your inner looks: will, confidence, humility.

The process of getting things done is mental break; you'll need to get down to the books.

If you're not already opening new doors, remember to close the others

By retracing what you've been working on for a while now.

Swindling is not going to get you anywhere.

The high road will probably be the best outcome.

Let that little voice in your head become the creator of your universe.

You've always worked hard on it.

Read the signs that'll bring grace and harmony back into your universe.

Now that'll be days worthy.

Carry on young soul

Even though there's a four way intersection;

At some point you'll make the right turn eventually someone will beep.

Don't cause any more crashes, please.

He is more powerful than he's ever been

This journey has been about a change of who's in charge: a more
powerful person in tune with the higher power, sketching a powerful
universe for the roads to arrive at, building the next chapter of his climax,
as he is willing to work out the cons of the past and turn into the pros of
the future.
If today is not the hardest, imagine tomorrow.
Traveling through this world without the will to be completely fine,
Wanting to pick up a few drinks
To cope with this inner circle of changes
Having those made decisions for you because you were at a standstill of
past memories that lead to a horrible habit.
If today is not the hardest, try thinking of tomorrow.

Who is making the decision for him? If today is not the hardest,
Imagine tomorrow. Dwelling on safety.
Jeopardizing his will of a shelter Avoiding a conflict that the helper has
made him a victim of
Can you bring me some help he asks for his higher power?
Is this a written test on self-will?
Is it a matter of standing up for oneself? Confused with this answer.
If today is not the hardest, Imagine tomorrow.
1,000-piece puzzle

At a standstill with a missing piece. Did he drop it?
A hundred-piece puzzle.
He's still missing three pieces
To complete this wholesome image.

Did he drop it?

Did he throw it away? Ooh wait!

Count to three Wait,

Found it!

Changes are grasping for the future.

333 (Good, good, bad)

The souls that keep belittling you are the Devil.

He's trying to mask the reality of what's actually conspiring right in front
of your eyes.

A thought process, an inner emotional roller coaster.

From happy highs to six feet under sadness.

A personal note definitely for the books. If the mess he had picked up just
became the breaking point in an already incomplete growth, what is his
weakness? Traveled the world wondering if the death day should come
sooner, or when the heart wants to stop.

From trying to figure out who's actually more of a butcher to his already
weak

Soul, perhaps his symphony can play one last time before the crowds gives

one more "boo."

66

Falls into a profound depression

In a Great Depression with changeable actions
Knowing it's easier said than done His mind
His Battlefield
His everyday war within his everyday thought
How can he seek help this time?
When does death become a selfish act? Fights with an inner demon that
brought about mounds of restless evenings?
Sometimes where you are, thinking it's your worst it's not.

Smile

A smile comes from the imagination of two dots and a hanging line
Simple right?
Find your other dot so they chill with you
Above your hanging line.

Take me home country roads

It's time to approach a new home for this not-so-settled soul
With the hopes of finding stability
With the hopes of finding the faith he needs.

The confidence in himself became a self-imposed turnout.

Never become a product of the past remains
Become the future of your own kind. The greatest.
Fluttering with the winds, the heart is gifted with fortunes, happy yeses
and great starts.

Regrets and somber tears.

His personality processed a
Traumatized past to create an outlook of rainy days,
Windy thoughts, and damaged paths.

73
Created war and bloodshed that ended unexpectedly.

Can change, a destructive path of conflict, really be the key to your
success? If life was as simple as a straight line, the heartbeat of your
broken dreams would stay at one point and the mirrors of your own
reflection would always reflect the same progression.
Gosh this is annoying

The tides are picking up washing ashore a lot of new beginnings.
Shells, Rocks, Seaweed,

And Wood

The tides move in, washing away a lot of the new beginnings.

75

He doesn't judge right away. Maybe it's his deficiency? Chill.

If the beginning of his time hasn't already created a conflicted master

mind in disguise, waiting for the wrath of his

60

Enemies to bring upon the evil eye to destroy the shelter he's created
Little do they realize, the climax to every story goes down with a plot twist
to some sort of not-so-happy ending.
Don't become the product of his universe if the universe doesn't work well
with your "life style."
An evil eye,
He's felt a few times
The shield of his broken glass.
Will never be the glass that you were trying to break.
77
Bam mother fucker.

Find him a peacemaker for his kingdom
As he goes to war with your enemies. A one-man operation.
Defending and defeating every opponent,

Mastering every obstacle, Producing his surroundings,

Self-aware of his daily emotional drive,

Power to the enemy,

Find him a peacemaker for his kingdom.

As he goes to war with your enemies, self-sabotaging is his focus.

Situations that are at a up most easy

Level of some scared failure overlooked his timeline

Find him a peacemaker for his kingdom, As he goes to war with the enemies, Only to realize the enemies are just phases of him that he had faded out.

79

Lol it's the only war that'll kill you faster than a cigarette

He once was a soul that bore a heavy shoulder Slouched down;

The clouds singing "oh rainy day."

He once was a soul where the reasons of an "are you ok" situation were

sprung upon him, by them or by him. He would answer with a simple

"okay" or a simple

"Aw I'm sorry." Paid no heed.

A battered mindset with the ability to create a good mindset

That was on the verge of going to waste, Until oh, His happy days began

to be seen Over the horizon.

The memories of his past have come to an end.

It's time for his stigma to start the fight It's time for his morals to become

what he wants to portray to the company he keeps while trying to create a

symbol for his universe

An expansion onto his followers, even those fillers in time.

His weary mind knows how to correct, the daily forgotten personal notes

he's made.

He didn't understand the concept of emotions,

Battered with a bleeding heart, drowning in his own tear drops, sucked in

by others' opinions.

Just because he wasn't sure if his own opinion was even validated—

without evening speaking about the topic,

81

Just brushing it away just like a broomstick dusting away a "dust bunny."

He always remembers his soul saying,

"To know how you feel, is to stick by what you want."

Life begins to write; stories—volumes

Pages that turn into chapters, Never a complete story,
But, a climax nonetheless.

"Tomorrow if I died there will be more of you
Tomorrow if I'm alive there will be less of you
Know yourself before your mind starts to want the attention and your
heart the emotion."
83
Between the stars and the moon is his home
Where the records of his past Are left strewn
Where
His footsteps walked His love for his family His love for his friends His
love for partner

His love for his animals Was his daily routine That didn't last long Lost family bonds

Lost his fur babies

Lost decades of old friendships

Lost good love stories

The actions of his broken past always became problems

High levels of stress

Night-owl settings

Daylight turned out to be restful hours

The night owl is him

A universe of beautiful lights Brisk walks

Coffee walks and talks

He begins to daze into the night sky

He sees a shooting star

A joy of hope, as they say

Between the stars and the moon

Is where the courses of his daily lessons that created a traumatized
mindset is now coming to rest.
Tear drops of understanding himself—happiness.
Between the stars and the moon He can come to terms
With a new beginning.

85

Dear father,
You've raised me when mother wasn't present, gave me a childhood, a
home, food on my plate, and clothes on my back—morning, noon, and

Night. Dear father, I am haunted by the pain you've endured for me.
I've caused outbursts because you've always kept me locked away,
Most of the time, I was the victim of your worst anger.
Physically remembering, mentally forgetting the next day, as step-mom
would always say, "Tomorrow's a new day."
Dear father, when your anger got the best of you
I would always think you want me gone. Dear father, I pray for your
sorrows now, I call once in a blue moon,
Just so I know, you're still alive.

87

Remember yourself, because it's you that lies every day, not them.

Them:
Bloodline.

The reason:

He spoke in volumes resulting in His daily dose of mattering.

The question:
Was wanting a new beginning, a new environment, or such a dramatic journey?

The feeling:
Finesse

If Life is all about overwhelming growth, why do we have an end date?

He valued his self-worth, his talent, and the meaning of what pride means
to him. Without knowing the abilities of his confidence,
He wakes up without any plan or action, which has created a fictional
character.

At times, life isn't so willing to fulfill a goal you've been trying for.

If life was easy,
Like always getting a yes for an answer, how boring would your days be?

Read all about it

I was a child. My abuser knew about the abilities of my self-worth. He tried to tarnish my mindset by saying I worth was nothing but dust on the floor.
Just a quick sweep.
It turned me into a person prone to a lot of drama as I began my adulthood.
Lost connections, stories, and memorable memories of people, places, and things.
Happy times, gone before I could eventually understand what people were saying.
It turned the people, places, and things into my worst trauma.
I'll have to live with this mindset till the day my heart stops beating and the thoughts that rush through my mindset finally go to sleep.

When I was a child, my abuser tried to convince me that I was worth
nothing but dust on the floor.
He lost.
I won.

As I rewrite my starlit sky

Shooting for another change, of course I was easily convinced the
impossible was such a drastic step. Resentment, anger, and fear, crossed
my mind. Shooting for another change, of course I was the impossible
drama queen. Life is flawed, you know?

It's Possible

I traveled a hundred miles to find a better beginning.
I took the steps, repaired my broken
Glass door
It created paths for new folks,
Subtle changes, heavy shifts, and uncomfortable tears that left a world of
pain, anger, and despair. The world I once endeavored, is now the reality
of my future.
It will be faced with obstacles, mazes, even risks.
Part three...

The reason you gave up

Blank spaces rushed through my head As emptiness became noticed

Lost torn

Shaken up I'm still breathing in a

World that isn't

Mine. I have walked down the paths of destruction and suffocation.

The truth lies

To you in a way that makes your scars become your daily fears.

To reflect on my past

I had to find my regrets, emotional battles, and fears. It became uncomfortable when I realized "It's okay, it's not okay?"

The world will bring you down stomp on your pride
Destroy your future
Just don't forget Happiness Pride is convenient, but
Your landslide doesn't matter.

Beggar, the man downtown

Was useless, cruel, and slandered. He was just torn into pieces.

Daily Dose Two

Written and Directed by:

Abuse.

It makes you repeat patterns.

Only when you're in full force in the stage of I-need-it-right-now,

Will you know closure.

Coping 101

As I sit and reflect on my inabilities, I forget my strengths and my ability
to foresee obstacles. My past has made me stronger.
I realize the me.
I'll add a catchy title to this new chapter, you'll see.

The cosmic bang

I left my better self to be with you, overcoming the worst in my mind, to
listen to your heart, to give you a better destination.

I hope I learn to get over myself

To be the master of my sea,
I'm preparing for desperate beginnings
Opening a destiny of letting go of the past While trying to settle the time
of a broken due date.
To be the master of my sea,

I'm preparing for desperate beginnings As I shred the tears from my weathered past.

"God damnit, Rachel."

His emotion is a stone. Not a single teardrop. Not a single smile. Not a single emotion.

Just a hard-headed person

With the inability to complete tasks

With his mind as crazy as rush-hour traffic

He laughs at the meaning of relaxation, "One day at a time"

His emotion is a stone

He doesn't fit in with the others

The rushing of his brain

People look at him

As if he's an object of self-hatred

Worthless love
A careless human they say
They don't want to create a life with him
He cries to those who've been in his life since the day his heart started to
beat
A complete shock moment every time
He is stuck
He is frozen
Is life in turmoil?

"Belittling those who hurt him
Two wrongs don't make a right
It's his life, let him figure it out,
Right?"
Bad days come back. The days of

Growth Lessons

As if he hasn't already gone through enough change

Here we go again...

Straight to the point. Not a mystery on site. His rush for importance

Is a simple impulsive movement Expressing more needs

With the mind as crazy. As rush-hour traffic

He's over an "I drink wine" kind of melody

As if he doesn't know His life's more important

Than the rush of such nonsense

He's tasted his own ownership because he gave

His world to some folks

That just sucked him bone-dry without even a respectful goodbye.

This is where it gets deeper...

Rated R

Today's feature

The word stupid. You're empty with dopamine,

Your only way of coping is "doing what's

Right"

Based on people, places, things. Emotional dominance is your form of

protection

While ego is to mask the open-door policy you supposedly portray.

You then travel into a lifeless cycle of hatred, regret, and resentments.

You question yourself knowing the outcome before it's even presented.

Just to revisit the animosity of your life.

Cool.

Mind Boggling
The cycle of always giving back, it starts with happiness,
The ending appears to creep up quickly. Annoyed
Mad at self

Disregard your personal wealth. Targeted by weakness.
Left to one side.

Worthless.

The walkaway

Ever heard yourself walk away from your body?

The first sign of "pitching a pity party"

Has begun howling at your own pack to seek the emotional damages they left.

Your scar that hurt your process of trying to be more socially acceptable during the simplest of occurrences?

Yeah, PTSD is forever a "claimant." The claimant will always create a scene.

Ever heard yourself walk away from your body? Ah.

Once it's called again

When the world is walking into you, your type of emotional response, the
mask of resentment,
Is the unintentional ignorance of the truth that you are masking.
Now you're on a window display for the action of judgment, to self-
destruct.

The daily routine of trying to erase the scar of a once-traumatic event that makes you feel like the world is talking too loud.

Poetic Vincent   35

You question yourself knowing the outcome before it's even presented.
Just to revisit the animosity of your life. Cool.
Roaming charges are increasing

Thursday, July 27, 2023
The well-being of asking for help

Leading to a "yes" mentality—By the people you scan through,
Seeking the easy road while the scanning process of "asking for help"
Is ruining your growth,
The emotional connection between them and you: you are not even trying
to
Take the steps of trying on your own.
We seek the easy way out—the process of trying alone to get what one
wants.
An uncomfortable journey taught by people, places, and things. We
just don't want to experience it again.

36   Poetic Vincent

Memory maker

When all you wanted to do is to enjoy a new memory,

That brings to the surface a new feature that you never thought you could

feel.

The days within always must carry some type of emotional baggage, of his

people, places, and things. He responds to range, in a hostile tone at him,

and them. All he is trying to do is enjoy a new memory with his memory

maker. Then again, they are just trying to ruin the small percentage of

happiness that he and others beg to see.

Roaming status; pending.

One of my defects is seeking a "shoulder to cry on..."

One of my fights is seeking a "shoulder to cry on..."

One of my journeys is to overcome a trip to experience

Poetic Vincent   37

A memory worth sharing while trying to compare
Toward a helpful hint in finding this middle meaning
This journey with the scar is giving rise to tornadoes. I'm losing too many
things.
Things—my people

PTSD, it's just ptsd

Sightseeing Aroma Sniff
(onomatopoei
A) Effects
Tactile imagery
Does it bring up a flashback?

If so,

This is called PTSD.

Caused by your people, places, and things.

Poetic Vincent   39

Oui.

Last night I asked my friend,

Why is it that I get told "It's so much drama..."

While explaining a question that they asked? He looked at me with tears.

40   Poetic Vincent

I am not Snow White

As you assume based on my daily tasks, swag, outlook, and

accomplishments—

I entertain my ego.

Am I a spoof of people, places, and things?

Nighttime creeps upon the weary man

Hoping for a quick chat with folks he comes across

Nighttime creeps upon the weary man hoping for a quick chat

A hopeful friendship is available upon purchase.

2023 society update: empty empathy

We walk around as if we know the meaning of the word love.

If we didn't, there would be no love

Stories.

Poetic Vincent   41

The climax of this assumed depressed soul. Played your games that you thought you could do better at
I won even before they could say "ready set go." Not even the ego came to light.
But your eyes were way more noticeable than the rising of those eyebrows upon the shocking results of my abilities.

I see that evil eye on your hateful faces.

Soon i'll be the mogul you'll need to purchase. Don't become a prey to me,
I like to fish,

Once it's time for gutting, That won't be me,

As you try to destroy your own pride, by thinking
Your words are effective,
I believe the winners will be announced.

To be present or not

Just because they said no, don't go crying, Wolf.

Life will always continue. We are just memories.

Match with high egos, become a purpose.

Idk anymore.

Getting used to a new custom

Built by a version of yourself that seeks a better you.

Seems to be backstabbing. Deeper and deeper into my back. Getting used

to a certain custom, while meeting hopefully at new beginnings has made

me

Poetic Vincent   43

More unpopular.

Always remind him of your disclaimer
As he simmers through the processes of your thoughts. He warned you of
his plans.
Don't act soapy.

When his karma comes to your attention.

I am your daily reminder.

As I become your morning routine thoughts
Your evil spell is restrained by my intelligence. See with me,
Rare is my new favorite character, To be different,
To be talked about, And to be hated.
Ever heard of reverse psychology?

44   Poetic Vincent

Her majesty once said, "Look what you made me do."

Yea that's right, that's my table.

Not yours.

To be talked about is to win
As I left the nest,
I started to explore the world, which I thought was to create, shelter, food,
and medical aid.
Imagine the simplicity of the three major keys to everyday living.
As I left the nest,
Poetic Vincent   45

I thought yes, I'm finally free.

"Such a force of freedom was expressed." If life could have been handed
to you,
I'm sure I would have performed the
"selfish act" already.

Remember you, when you ask yourself why you want to end you
They provided legal documentation to move forward.
He lamented before them with low esteem, "It takes two tangs."
Distraught thoughts, they formed a tighter group. They found the power
to end him, nicely, they thought.
The people, places, and things.
Watch for the tone, the action, and how they view "the boy who cried
wolf..."

They provided legal documentation to move forward; the case got thrown
out.
Reverse psychology to the point. Imagine being so insecure!
You tried to make a game plan that convinced the people that could
potentially make his life be taken away.
Imagine being so sure the game planned will be completed. Never
underestimate   someone's   worth
Based off your self-worth.
It just ends with the victim becoming a suspect.

I am the power to my name, don't create false facts
They pressed him on pending charges.
The people, places, and things turned on him, as if the press knows
anything about accuracy.
They pressed him on pending chargers. He knew it was all intended,
The   people,   places, and things.
Now they must beg for his forgiveness.

Yet
The people, places, and things Are all his muse.
Yet,

The Catch-22 is,

They easily create triggering attacks.

Pride is now his craft
If the world had an end date,

Then it would already have completed its course. Becoming self-aware
of his own pride,
Has become the mastery of his craft.

He can tell the stories that led up to this achievement, Understand:
There's always an evil eye that expels
Just don't become their product.

Poetic Vincent   49

If he consumed your thoughts, probably he proved the point of He is he,
no one can break him. Type of melody,
As you try to reach for his downfalls He is right on top.
Overlooking your lack of insight with incomplete information
That has zero relevance to any type of tragedy you thought you would
create for his ending.
He is him that no one can cancel.

As you try to reach for his downfalls He is right on top
Overlooking the timeline of memories you both had within each other.
Never questioning.

Just glancing with a smile of "Oh happy days."

Advertisement: anyone?
Starting to devalue my self-

Esteem based on people, places, and things.
Becoming the central focus

The all-eyes-on-you type of guy

As I start to devalue my self-esteem.

I'm just trying to figure out the chain to my rhythm. To the root, to when
it all began.
You allow it to happen – mind reset. 100% complete. The past days, the
world has been in charge of his mindset.
He self-destructs into a pit full of his own pity parties
Created with people, places, and things. Just imagine how his mind set it
today - Embarrassed,
Shocked, grateful.
Poetic Vincent   51

Yea, gratitude was the purpose of the pity parties. These weeklong pity
parties,
Were created for the findings of how he is to destroy his own
Ego—with people, places, and things.

You get what you get—idk. Ignorance comes from the
Three seasons—fall, winter, and summer. Never spring.
It's the climax to any story. Everything comes back to life —I mean,
That's the   Catch-22   in

Everything.

Fuck You
Walking through the forest of invalid information that you gave me to
find my way back home,

I started to hurtle into an angry, confused, and scared state of mind,
where the things around became interesting, along with the concern of
my aura that I was beaming.
Walking through the forest of invalid information that you gave me
turned me into a monster of trust issues, jealousy, and the fear of losing
my state of being marked with scars after I made it home.

Poetic Vincent   53

He is starting to create a name that will live on in history,
For the world to see as a limelight on the inner thoughts of our
conversations of pure, self-hatred filled, selfish thoughts, and to prove to
ourselves that we are more than just our names.
Yet it starts with knowing the seed that created the roots of the legacy
you're supposed to carry on with or without your sightseeing of people,
places, and things.
Carrying yourself with dignity doesn't mean becoming a follower.
Become the creator to show your following you can always be the leader
and become a cause, for the good.
Expect the evil,

Always leave your remorse up to the universe. He is creating a name that
will live on in history. The name is Poetic Vincent.
The writer that speaks through triggers.

Everybody wants something.
Imagine if the world wanted your attention? Imagine nine billion people.

Know your people, places, and things. Yea, even the fucked-up part. Remember, hated by many and loved by very few?

The circle you need has to be small, the circle also needs to be large. Enemies fuel your fire, charisma, and stigma. Correct me if I'm wrong?

Poetic Vincent 55

Friday, August 25, 2023

How would you design the city of the future?

The most profound song in world history goes a little like "Almost heaven

West Virginia, blue-ridge mountains…"

More into the song it goes…

"…life is old there, Olden than trees…"

We are moving too fast, creating imagery that has already been done, or

we are shunned by such groups labels, you name it, "I guess."

To answer honestly, The old way,

The way of trusting,

Teaching unconditional love, unconditional family values, just be home

with your family or what you call your family.

Life is so short, especially nowadays. Trust thy neighbor, or find thy neighbor.

56   Poetic Vincent

The world is big.

Boy oh boy!
Don't call me a narcissist if you know my self-worth. I am not the mirror
to your insecurities.
It's your judgement based upon your ignorance that brings up the evil
eye, nonsense scenarios that don't have to happen.

Poetic Vincent 57

Sunday, August 27, 2023

What's your favorite recipe?

To answer in Poetic Vincent language:
They can't claim they held your hand through the struggles when the
only hand that was being held was the one on the left as you put right
and left side together.
You then began to ask for help, guidance, and some truth during these
sinking times.
To find some helpful melodies—so this.

I guess the world hasn't had different days
Easy isn't the way I want you to portray your stigma when you first meet
me.
Create an unknown stigma.

He likes to understand the unknown. It creates a new stigma for his
people, places, and things.

Pour your heart out without even speaking! Cry him melody so he can change!

58   Poetic Vincent

Make a rainbow to show some hope at the end. It's all he asks of.

Sometimes telling yourself to be subtle

Will attract the opposite of what you are wanting. The key word is
"wanting."
Wanting is for the unknown, (people, places, and things are
Thriving off the evil eye that are portrayed by both sides?) Yes, both sides.
Imagine this – you're in a fight with people, places, and things. Plot twist:
I didn't know about the evil eye and evil acts that are portrayed before
me, thrust upon me.
Guess when they say make sure you have a "killer" climax. They're not
wrong...
Poetic Vincent   59

This is PTSD talking

I'm praying for the days ahead that will bring about an at-ease mindset of finding some kind of way to make the people, places. And things. That won't rush my end date.

Praying for the days of some kind of solid healing for my body at least. I am beautiful.

The insides are slowly tarnishing away.

The daily reporter reported that his cause of grief is yet to be determined.

I'm sorry I didn't relapse, I'm just mentally ill. It's called attacks.

I believe my pacing has to do with my anxiety, I'm sorry. It's not a relapse.

Ask my old people, places, and things.

60   Poetic Vincent

Again, another questionable decision by the new people, places, and things.
Yet you check upon my privacy now by turning it backwards on me?
With some alleged errors?
I'm sorry I haven't relapsed.

Damn.
I have so much taken away from me, and the evil eye still surrounds me with its daily urges that are becoming routine.

Thursday, August 31, 2023

What daily habit do you have that improves your quality of life?
There's a new remedy I saw on The Today Show—The tapping, three
taps on certain parts of the body.
It's helped me cut down on cigarettes. Anxiety,
And lately my personal experiences (broadly).

The bitter symphony of broken hearts. Life is good when your heart breaks.

Life is good when your mind goes full throttle

And you're now pouring tears of rain caused by their "revenge conspiracies."

Yea, conspiracies I mean at this point,

It's so believable that my people, places, and things are the only so-called astrologist.

Poetic Vincent

Thursday, August 31, 2023

64   Poetic Vincent

What's your favorite time of the day?
Nighttime – the world is resting, no one to be seen, I mean… "Once and
blue moon, you'll see someone…"
The imagery's response is Shaky – morning
Thoughts – overthinking after noon
Ego – nights wondering soul, those who are up. Are those who not his
company to keep.
Rephrase "PHEW"

They're just back at the old people, places, and things.

•

P.P.T

Friday, September 01, 2023

He sees the fictional stories that have fallen from his people, places, and
things. Shaking body,
Rushing through his task while outside

His safe space,

He sees the fictional sorrows that are waiting to be told to him.
He just wishes for nonfictional sorrows instead.

Friday, September 01, 2023

How are you feeling right now?
Oui—trying to communicate within myself to convince myself that
people, places, and things aren't out to get me. In other words, it's hard
for me to expect compassion and empathy.
Yes or no, Vincent?

To end a long two-months of utter chaos, realism, and inner peace,
I found myself engaging more with the no aspects. I thought those
months were my end.
Life can be such a great place for you to become your own

People, places, and things. While trying to seek no evil revenge or
reasoning from such past traumatic catastrophes,
You come to realize the power of giving people, places, and things the
benefit of their own doubts. You can define your own position in life by
letting go of past errors.
Don't go into every conversation, downfall, heart ache, or dive with the
only stigma you know.
To end a long two months of utter chaos, realism, and inner peace,
I found myself engaging more in the no aspects.

The Boxer
Sometimes when life throws curve balls, even non-goalies score goals.
We undermine the stigma we are wanting change.
Poetic Vincent   67

Self-growth Validation Success?

The meaning behind these hardwired questions turns our minds into emotional wreckage. We then seem to seek out to find the answer, "help?" Again, sometimes life throws curve balls, and non- goalies miss getting into the net.

Pause and remember the stigma you're trying to fight against.

68   Poetic Vincent

I'm not sure what this chapter will be called. Better yet, to take away the
suspense,
Think of it like this,

He cried wolf to people, places, and things. Clear as day
They tip-toed away. Tried to persuade the evil, in a self-sabotaging way.
You know, the victim turning into the suspect. Yea, that.
Saturday, September 09, 2023
How do you relax?
Answering in Poetic Vincent mindset:

—

You can't express a thought of the underlying past troubles. Imagine:
moving forward is like saying no,
LOL, "point blank?" While sitting with oneself,
Shut down what's around you? Laugh, tear, and smile.
You already passed the anger of the thought of going
Backwards,

Now with this subtle mindset moving forward. Relax,
Just laugh, tear jerk, smile? Oui.
To smile is to create laughter, to tear jerk is to understand, what
underlying emotions bring to the relationship with the word relaxation.
It's only a relationship, you have to carry you know, "Be stuck with"
Why?

It's the product of "who you are."

So how do I relax? Finding the core to:

Who I am.

What personality trait in people is a red flag for you? Is safety at, fuck
that's about 98% of yes.

People mistake karma. Karma defined: a higher power will
Take control of such evil. Gods got this.
Karma isn't a physical form. It's mental.
Now, let's try again. Yea? Grit—is to find.
You don't see grit, tip toe away. It's not easy. Just to walk away
From.

Rage Unveiled
I am not depressed. I'm angry.
I am not selfish. I'm angry.
If a person, place, or thing makes you feeling like the end of
Yourself, correct thy self.
I'm the type of person who

"No Vincent, you're a baddie..." I am not depressed,
I'm angry. I am not

Selfish,

I am angry.

Dwelling on the same topic constantly? It's time for a new chapter, you know? The chapter is so long,

It has become a series.

Again, what are my people, places, and things? I am not depressed.

I'm angry.

I am not selfish. I'm angry.

Wednesday, September 13, 2023

I don't seek an emotional response from my daily complaints. Just needs to be heard.

Don't justify my tone either.

It's just your stigma that you can't seem to change about yourself.

Please.

Poetic Vincent   73

Dear, the company I kept —

As the restful hours came to an end,

I expelled my colleagues from the burning office. As if it's the price they
paid me hourly.
Was it even worth it? Some walked back in, looking back with such
disgust. Ha!
As the restful hours came to an end, I tried to expel my colleagues from
the burning office.
They just thought I was crying wolf.

74   Poetic Vincent

Carry

I'll use it in a sentence or Poetic Vincent's mind.

He carries himself with a burden, a heartache, a relapse, and dignity.

Imagination isn't the sadness.

That would be his favorite word, "carry."

Always carry yourself with a purpose even if the burdens are destroying

your soul.

The heartache will come to an end. I promise.

Poetic Vincent   75

Rising Above Adversity
The Brilliance of His Name
Grow his name!
Like the daily topics that come out of your mouth. He slays the woe of
burdens.
As if he asks for some type of emotional support from anyone,
His abyss already feeds off the thought of His accusers.
Practice the words that make him your daily topic! He is too brilliant.

JOKER

76   Poetic Vincent

You brought out your scared remedies.

Now, is that just dust in the wind?

As if you were taught that the dust in the wind somehow comes back?

Oui

"Woosh woosh!" Sweetheart, why so scared? Why so tense?

That's right,

They're clapping because of my   ability.Not   our nonsense.

One day onward, we will never be forgotten. That's the day we will make
history.
Now, start small. Work your way up,
Again, if the same repeating

Patterns continue, ask yourself: is it really meant to be?
The people, place, and things.
They compromised his privacy and spoke about his illness, with their
hearts purely pushing him away,
Again, if the same repeating

Patterns continue, ask yourself: is it really meant to be?
But the emotional response was a calm sense of relief?

I'm pretty sure that you reached your milestone a year ago. You just
haven't found your home yet.
It's ok, just remember,

He knows.

Mindfulness

The cycle of always giving back,
It starts with happiness,
The ending seems to creep up quickly
Annoyed
Mad at self
Disregarding my own personal wealth.
Targeted by weakness
Left to the side, once
Worthless.

The walk away

Ever hear yourself walk away from your body?
The first sign of "pitching a pity party"
Has begun
Howling to your own pack to seek the emotional damages they left.
Your scar overwhelms your process of trying to be more socially
acceptable during the simplest of occurrences?
Yeah, PTSD is forever a "claimant"
And the claimant will always present a scene. Ever hear yourself walk
away from your body?

This is my skill

I retain wars with people, not anything that somebody said or some form
of physical harm.
It's the doubt of my ambition I talk about
It's a lack of interest in "who I am."

Yet, lust is your wondering eye.
It's the doubt of my grace
It's "a slap in the face", a circumstance
That makes me look at you with zero feeling of denial—when somebody
hears that tone of judgment.
The powerful stigma of yourself is beyond my story pages; I'm just not in
the mood to battle myself
I completed that milestone; thanks, tho.

Please

As I beg for a new beginning
Away from where it all started
I forgot what's it's like to live, laugh, and love
In order it make some changes to this system, i must become noticeably
I must surrender myself to the people, places, and things.
I've given up all my powers, abilities, and forces.
Now i've rewritten my timeline
Would anyone be, like, buddies or family?

I'm falling into solemn depression.

His world is now the feeling of success
He becomes the power to his name,
Daily bypasses of helping anyone, a simple smile or even "hey what's
up....?"
He's overcoming the people, places, and thing
By letting go of the frustration and hatred he's given them—
Ya know: the EVIL EYE!
The sounds of the melody are in the backdrop
He is now becoming at ease—with the people, places, and thing.

Growth

I was once a seed,
During the worst months of the great American drought—
Every chance I had,
I tried to get a little sip.
From when the weatherman said "the chances of rain are low, but there's
still hope!" I held on,
A year later the great American drought ended

And brought up, a beautiful yet new flower.

Elegant as the summer rays.

We would like to thank Editage.com for editing and reviewing this manuscript for English language.

www.ingramcontent.com/pod-product-compliance
Lightning Source LLC
Chambersburg PA
CBHW021534150726
47990CB00006B/2234